YOU CHOOSE
BOOKS ™

WORLD WAR II
INFANTRYMEN

An Interactive History Adventure

by Steven Otfinoski

Consultant:
Dennis Showalter, PhD
Professor of History
Colorado College

CAPSTONE PRESS
a capstone imprint

You Choose Books are published by Capstone Press,
1710 Roe Crest Drive, North Mankato, Minnesota 56003
www.capstonepub.com

Library of Congress Cataloging-in-Publication Data
Otfinoski, Steven.
  World War II infantrymen : an interactive history adventure / by Steven Otfinoski.
  p. cm.—(You choose. World War II)
  Includes bibliographical references and index.
  Summary: "Describes the role infantryman played during World War II. Readers' choices reveal
various historical details"—Provided by publisher.
  ISBN 978-1-4296-9964-8 (library binding) — ISBN 978-1-62065-716-4 (pbk.)
  ISBN 978-1-4765-1811-4 (eBook PDF)
  1. World War, 1939–1945—Campaigns—Philippines—Juvenile literature. 2. World War, 1939–
1945–Campaigns–Africa, North—Juvenile literature. 3. World War, 1939–1945—Campaigns—
France—Normandy—Juvenile literature. 4. Infantry—History—20th century—Juvenile
literature. [1. World War, 1939–1945—Campaigns—Philippines. 2. World War, 1939–1945—
Campaigns—Africa, North. 3. World War, 1939–1945—Campaigns—France—Normandy.
4. Infantry.] I. Title. II. Title: World War 2 infantrymen.
  D743.7.O74 2013
  940.54′1—dc23   2012029956

Editorial Credits
Jennifer Besel, editor; Bobbie Nuytten, designer; Wanda Winch, media researcher;
Jennifer Walker, production specialist

Photo Credits
Alamy: DIZ Muenchen GmbH, Sueddeutsche Zeitung Photo, 57; AP Images: U.S. Army, 12;
Capstone, 6 (maps); Corbis, 28, Bettmann, 21, 22; Courtesy of the Council of the National Army
Museum, London, 44, 49, 54, 63; Courtesy of Ingrid Dockter, dog tag design element; National
Archives and Records Administration, 40, Army Signal Corps Collection, 80, 84, U.S. Army
photo, 70, 100, U.S. Army photo: 2nd Lt. Jacob Harris, 105, U.S. Army photo: Maj. Paul Wing,
36, U.S. Coast Guard, 75, U.S. Navy, 86; Newscom: akg-images, 9; Shutterstock: Andrey Kuzmin,
metal plate design, Nella, metal texture; SuperStock Inc: SuperStock, cover

Printed in the United States of America in Brainerd, Minnesota.
092012   006938BANGS13

TABLE OF CONTENTS

About Your Adventure.......................... 5

Chapter 1
War Begins 7

Chapter 2
Heat in the Jungle 13

Chapter 3
Showdown in the Desert 41

Chapter 4
Invasion at Normandy 71

Chapter 5
The War Ends at Last 101

Timeline.. 106
Other Paths to Explore......................... 108
Read More 109
Internet Sites... 109
Glossary.. 110
Bibliography.. 111
Index 112

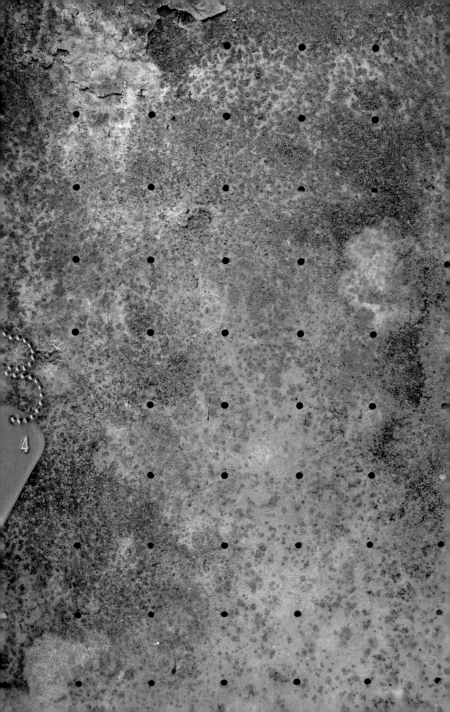

ABOUT YOUR ADVENTURE

YOU live in a world at war in the early 1940s. The Allies are fighting the Axis powers' attempt to take control of the world. What part will you play in the war?

In this book, you'll explore how the choices people made meant the difference between life and death. The events you'll experience happened to real people.

Chapter One sets the scene. Then you choose which path to read. Follow the directions at the bottom of each page. The choices you make will change your outcome. After you finish one path, go back and read the others for new perspectives and more adventures.

YOU CHOOSE the path
you take through history.

EUROPE

ATLANTIC OCEAN

NORWAY
SWEDEN
FINLAND
L. Ladoga
Rybinsk Res.
Gulf of Finland
ESTONIA
Kuybyshev
North Sea
DENMARK
LATVIA
SOVIET UNION
Baltic Sea
LITHUANIA
IRELAND
EAST PRUSSIA
NETH.
U. K.
BELGIUM
GERMANY
POLAND
Bay of Biscay
SLOVAKIA
SWITZERLAND
HUNGARY
FRANCE
ROMANIA
ITALY
Adriatic Sea
Black Sea
PORTUGAL
YUGOSLAVIA
BULGARIA
SPAIN
Tyrrhenian Sea
GREECE
Aegean Sea
TURKEY
TUNISIA
CYPRUS
LEBANON

| ALLIED CONTROLLED | AXIS CONTROLLED | NEUTRAL NATIONS |

ASIA

SOVIET UNION
MONGOLIA
MANCHURIA
PACIFIC OCEAN
KOREA
CHINA
JAPAN
TIBET
NEPAL
BHUTAN
BURMA
BANGLADESH
THAILAND
VIETNAM
FRENCH INDOCHINA
PHILIPPINES
INDIA
SRI LANKA
BRUNEI
MALAYSIA
SINGAPORE
BORNEO
SUMATRA
NEW GUINEA
NETHERLANDS INDIES

WORLD WAR II,
ALLIED AND AXIS TERRITORIES
IN EUROPE AND ASIA

WAR BEGINS

It is early 1942, and the world is at war. Germany, Japan, and Italy have joined forces. Together they have invaded country after country. These three nations are known as the Axis powers. The Allies will do all they can do to stop the Axis powers. The Allies are the United States, United Kingdom, Soviet Union, China, and those fighting with them.

The problems that started this war began more than 20 years ago. The first World War lasted from 1914 to 1918. It ended in defeat for Germany. The winners, including the United States, France, and Great Britain, dealt harshly with Germany.

7

Turn the page.

Germany lost all its colonies after the war. Its size was reduced by one-eighth. Its army and navy were also greatly reduced. The German economy declined and unemployment soared.

An economic depression in the 1930s also affected much of the world. People in some European nations looked to strong leaders to restore their nations' greatness.

Benito Mussolini came to power in Italy in the 1920s. By 1933 Adolf Hitler and his Nazi Party had control of Germany. Hitler's goals were to establish a German empire and get rid of people he called "undesirables." These people included the Jewish population of Europe. In May 1936 Italy and Germany signed a pact to work together.

Hitler (right) welcomed Mussolini to Germany in June 1940.

In 1938 Hitler began to put his plans into action. In March Germany took control of Austria. By October, it occupied neighboring Czechoslovakia. When Hitler invaded Poland on September 1, 1939, Great Britain and France declared war on Germany.

In April 1940 German troops occupied Denmark and attacked Norway. The following month Germany invaded Belgium and the Netherlands.

Turn the page.

By June 1940, France had fallen to the Germans. Italy invaded British African colonies in August and Greece in October. Japan invaded French territory in Asia in September. Meanwhile, Hitler set his sights on Great Britain. He launched an intensive air attack on the nation. But the British held out.

Frustrated, Hitler invaded Yugoslavia and joined Italy in attacking Greece in April 1941. Two months later, he turned on the Soviet Union, launching a major attack on that vast nation.

Then on December 7, 1941, Japan launched a sneak attack on the American naval base at Pearl Harbor in Hawaii. The next day the United States declared war on Japan. Days later the United States declared war on Japan's allies, Germany and Italy.

Right now it feels like the whole world is fighting. The Allies are battling the Axis powers in three major parts of the world—the islands in the Pacific Ocean, North Africa, and Europe. You have joined the army and will fight for your country in the infantry. Where will you fight?

• *To be an American infantryman in the Philippines, turn to page 13.*

• *To serve as a British soldier in North Africa, turn to page 41.*

• *To fight as an American soldier in the D-Day invasion in France, turn to page 71.*

U.S. soldiers ducked for cover in a foxhole as the Japanese attacked on the Bataan Peninsula.

CHAPTER 2

HEAT IN THE JUNGLE

It is January 1942. Last month the Japanese began landing troops in the Philippines. Now Japanese forces have taken over nearly all of the island nation. American and Filipino soldiers have retreated to the Bataan Peninsula.

You are among the American infantrymen defending Bataan. General Douglas MacArthur is your commander. On February 22 President Franklin Roosevelt orders MacArthur and his staff to evacuate so the Japanese won't capture them. From Australia, MacArthur sends a statement to the Filipinos promising, "I shall return."

13

Turn the page.

General Jonathan Wainwright is now in command of the Allied forces in the Philippines. He is a good leader, but you wonder how long he can hold out against overwhelming odds. The Japanese have the Americans and Filipinos bottled up on the Bataan peninsula.

The Japanese infantry is moving steadily forward. Food supplies are getting low on Bataan. Some of the men go into the jungle to hunt animals for food. They kill snakes, lizards, and monkeys. They even eat their own pack mules. The situation is growing desperate. It's only a matter of time before Bataan falls to the Japanese.

The island of Corregidor lies off the coast of Bataan. Wainwright is positioned on Corregidor, occupying an old Spanish fort called The Rock. He'll make his last stand there.

You could transfer to Corregidor before Bataan falls. There you could face a bloody battle, which you might not survive. But staying on Bataan and surrendering to the Japanese could bring an even worse fate. What will you do?

15

• To continue the fight on Corregidor, turn to page 16.

• To surrender to the Japanese at Bataan, turn to page 17.

You get your transfer to Corregidor. As the days pass, the Japanese step up their attack on the island. You and the other men flee to the long underground tunnel beneath the fort. Every time a shell lands on the fort, the ground shakes. Dirt and dust from the earthen ceiling fall on you.

On May 5 the Japanese come ashore on Corregidor and close in on the tunnel. General Wainwright fears there will be a last bloody battle. He urges the commanders still fighting outside the fort to surrender.

Many of your fellow soldiers are ready to surrender. But others plan to escape into the hills and continue fighting. You don't have much time to decide what to do.

• To flee to the hills, turn to page 25.

• To surrender, turn to page 36.

You surrender to the Japanese. You are one of more than 70,000 soldiers from Bataan who are now prisoners of war. The Japanese plan to march you 65 miles to the city of San Fernando. It quickly becomes clear that the Japanese will not be kind. They randomly beat you and the other prisoners.

You and two friends in your company, Frank and Tom, march in line with other prisoners. A truck pulls up on the dirt road. Inside sit rows and rows of Filipino prisoners. A Japanese guard climbs out of the truck's cab.

"We can take a few more," he says in English. Your friends shake their heads. These guards could be more cruel than the ones walking with you. But it is a long march to San Fernando.

• To keep marching, turn to page 18.

• To get in the truck, turn to page 20.

You decide against the truck, fearing what might happen if you leave the others. But you soon start to wonder if you made the right choice.

You march in rows of four. The hot sun beats down on you. You are tired from nights of little sleep and almost no food in the last days of the fighting. On top of that, the guards are cruel. One hit your head with the butt of his riffle.

You barely have the strength to lift your feet. Your body is bathed in sweat, and your throat burns with thirst. You ask one of the guards if you can have some water. He just smiles and dumps out a canteen of water on the ground in front of you.

You hear gunshots every now and then. But you are too focused on trying to walk to look at what or who is being shot. You can only think about water and rest.

Hours pass. It is late afternoon now, and it takes everything you have just to lift one foot after another. Finally you stumble on a root and fall.

"Get up," says Tom, holding out his hand and looking quickly over his shoulder.

You try to stand, but the ground feels soft and cool. Your body desperately needs rest. Lying here for just a few minutes would make you feel so much better. But will you be punished for falling behind?

19

• To get up and continue marching, turn to page 22.

• To stay on the ground and rest, turn to page 38.

You climb into the truck and wave good-bye to your friends. You promise yourself that you will find them later at San Fernando.

The ride is long and bumpy. But you're lucky. The guards driving this truck are kinder than others you've passed. Some other guards put a rope around a prisoner's neck and pulled him behind their truck. You push that image from your mind.

Late in the afternoon, the truck you're in gets stuck in the mud. The guards tell you and the others to get out and push. You all push hard, but the truck doesn't budge. The guards join you in pushing. You realize this might be the perfect time to escape into the jungle. But can you make it without getting caught?

American and Filipino prisoners of war were forced to march to the prison camp at San Fernando.

21

• *To make your escape, turn to page 28.*

• *To stay with the truck, turn to page 32.*

You take your friend's hand and force yourself to your feet. He looks greatly relieved. You hear more gunshots in the distance.

"What is that?" you ask.

"It's the clean-up squad," explains Tom. "They're shooting those who fall behind. I saw them shoot a man who fell down earlier."

You realize that shot could have been fired at you.

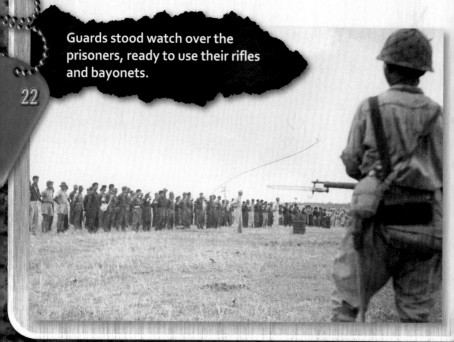

Guards stood watch over the prisoners, ready to use their rifles and bayonets.

22

Suddenly the march comes to a halt.
A Japanese officer is speaking to the prisoners.
He points to a nearby field.

"We will stay here for the night," he says.

Your captors wrap barbed wire around a group of trees. This will be your sleeping quarters. The Japanese herd you and the other prisoners behind the barbed wire like cattle.

You are given no food or water. You lie on the wet ground and listen to the moans of the men around you. Many of them are sick with malaria and dysentery. You vow that tomorrow you will escape this death march or die trying.

Turn the page.

In the morning you are awakened by a guard's rifle butt in your side. You line up with the other prisoners. You tell Frank and Tom about your plan to escape. You ask them to join you, but they shake their heads.

"It's too dangerous," says Frank. "You'll never make it."

"I've got to try," you tell them.

The march resumes. You are walking along a river. The bank is lined with tall grass. The guard in your outfit is distracted a few rows away. There may be no better time to make your move. But it's risky, and you may end up getting shot.

• To attempt an escape, turn to page 26.
• To stay with the marchers, turn to page 27.

You flee into the hills with other American soldiers before the surrender begins. The hills are steep, and soon you're panting in the heat. The jungle is so thick, and you're in such a rush to get away, that suddenly you're all alone. Where are your companions? A knot forms in the pit of your stomach. Maybe it was a mistake to escape.

It is getting late. The sun begins to sink. You have to decide what to do. Should you push on into the darkness to put more distance between you and the enemy? Or should you find a place to rest for the night?

25

• To keep going, turn to page 34.

• To rest for the night, turn to page 39.

The moment is right to make a break. You drop to the ground and roll away from the marching feet behind you. Other prisoners think you have fallen from fatigue and ignore you. As they pass, you roll into the tall grass along the riverbank.

You peer through the grass. Other groups of marchers are passing. Will one of the guards notice that you are missing from the line? You could dive into the river and cross to the other side, where you should be safer. Or is it better to wait until all the marchers have passed?

- To wait, turn to page 30.
- To dive into the river now, turn to page 35.

Your heart beats hard. You decide to wait. But as the day progresses, you find no better time to escape. The nearby guard has his eye on you. It's as if he knows what you're thinking.

One day blends into another. The guards are cruel. They beat and spit on the prisoners. They force you all to march in the hot sun with no rest. They give you no water or food. Your throat burns, and your thoughts spin. Some men are so desperate they dive for the dirty, muddy water on the side of the road. The guards shoot or stab anyone who steps out of the line.

After more than a week of this torture, you finally reach San Fernando. In all, only 54,000 of the 76,000 men who started the march finished it alive. And you are one of them. You have survived what will come to be called the Bataan Death March.

27

Turn to page 29.

You make your move. The guards are concentrating on the truck and don't see you sneaking into the jungle.

But the ground is muddy. The sucking sound of your boots in the mud attracts one guard's attention. He cries out. You run faster.

Suddenly two guards tackle you from behind. They tie you up with ropes and throw you on the floor of the truck.

After reaching San Fernando, prisoners were shipped in boxcars to Camp O'Donnell prison camp.

28

The San Fernando prison camp is a filthy place lined with barbed wire. You are jammed together with hundreds of other prisoners. Many of them are very sick. Guards toss the sickest men under the flooring of an old building, where they will soon die.

One evening the guards bring out large cans of rice. They begin to feed the men closest to the prison gates. You can almost taste the warm rice in your mouth. Then all at once, the guards take the cans away.

You are starving and exhausted. It feels as if you've been a prisoner for years, but it's only been a couple of weeks. But they have been the worst of your life. One morning you come down with malaria. You are soon burning with fever. When death nears, you look on it as a blessing. You will finally be free from this nightmare.

THE END
To follow another path, turn to page 11.
To read the conclusion, turn to page 101.

You decide to wait. You watch as the groups of marchers pass by. When they have all passed, you wade into the muddy waters of the river and swim across.

You climb out on the other side. Your clothes are soaked, but they dry quickly in the hot sun. The trail ahead leads deeper into the jungle. You were hoping to find friendly Filipinos who would help you. But you don't meet a soul.

As time passes you carve out a rough life for yourself. You make clothes from animal skins. You eat plants you find in the jungle and hunt animals with your bayonet. You even build a shelter not too far from Manila Bay. You think being close to the bay will give you the best chance of finding someone.

Every day you search for friendly Filipinos. One day you make your way to Manila Bay. You are shocked to find a band of Filipino guerrillas there.

"I've been living in the jungle since Bataan fell to the Japanese," you tell them.

"That was more than two years ago. It's 1944 now," one of the men tells you. You are stunned.

Then they give you the best news you've heard in a long time. "A few weeks ago, on October 20, MacArthur returned to the Philippines! He landed on the island of Leyte, southeast of here."

You breathe a sigh of relief. Soon MacArthur will lead the Allied forces to free the Philippines. You will finally be able to go home.

THE END
To follow another path, turn to page 11.
To read the conclusion, turn to page 101.

You decide not to risk an escape attempt. A few more minutes of pushing finally gets the truck out of the mud. You continue on your way.

In two days you arrive at the prison camp at San Fernando. It is a terrible place. You are locked in an area surrounded by barbed wire. In a few days the other prisoners begin to arrive on foot. Their eyes are hollow and their screams of pain and starvation never end. The guards crowd more than 1,000 other prisoners in with you. There are no bathrooms. Men have to relieve themselves right where they stand. Soon the smell becomes overwhelming.

Within the sea of faces, you see a soldier from your company. You shout to him and ask about your friends Tom and Frank. He pauses and swallows.

"They didn't make it," he says and turns away.

Your heart sinks. But maybe they're better off than being stuck in this filthy, horrible place.

Then one day the crowd starts moving. Guards force you and the other prisoners into boxcars. They shove more than 100 of you into a car that should only hold 25. Then they lock the doors. You have no idea where you're going or what might happen.

You think of your family back home and how much you miss them. You think of Tom's and Frank's families too. They don't know what's happened to their loved ones. You decide you must survive so that you can tell their families what happened. This alone will keep you going.

THE END

To follow another path, turn to page 11.
To read the conclusion, turn to page 101.

You decide to keep going. You'll put more space between you and the enemy, and it's cooler to travel by night. You step on grass that gives way under your weight. Suddenly you find yourself tumbling through space. You hit soft dirt and rise unsteadily to your feet. You have fallen into some kind of pit. Whether it was made by the Japanese or the Filipinos, you don't know. What you are sure of is that you are trapped.

You will sit and wait for morning, hoping that someone will rescue you. You pray that person is a friend and not an enemy.

34

THE END
To follow another path, turn to page 11.
To read the conclusion, turn to page 101.

You plunge into the river. The current is slow, and you swim with clean, confident strokes. You are in the middle of the river when you hear shots from the shore. Too late, you realize you should have waited. The guards heard the loud splash you made and have rushed to the riverbank. They are shooting at you.

The opposite shore is only a few yards away, but you will never make it there. You feel a sharp pain in your shoulder. Then a second bullet pierces your back. You sink below the muddy waters.

35

THE END

To follow another path, turn to page 11.
To read the conclusion, turn to page 101.

You and many other soldiers decide it's pointless to fight any longer. You ignore the whine of the falling shells and go to your underground barracks. You wash up, shave, and put on your best uniform. You will show the enemy that you are proud to be an American soldier.

As your captors lead you and the others out of the fort, you hear gunfire in the distance. Other soldiers outside the fort have ignored the order to surrender. They continue to fight the Japanese in foxholes.

Before the surrender, U.S. soldiers worked and lived in the underground tunnels at Corregidor.

The Japanese take you to a prison camp. You meet soldiers who surrendered at Bataan. A guy named John tells you hair-raising stories about the grueling 65-mile march they were forced to make.

"The Japanese soldiers beat us mercilessly. We couldn't even stop to use a bathroom."

"What happened if you tried?" you ask.

John drops his gaze. "They would kill you."

Camp life is harsh. Guards torture prisoners. Disease spreads like wildfire. So far you haven't caught anything. But you grow weak from the small rations of food. You cling to the hope that the Allies will win the war. If you're lucky, you'll still be alive to go home to your loved ones.

THE END

To follow another path, turn to page 11.
To read the conclusion, turn to page 101.

You stay on the ground. Your body is just too weak to go on right now. Tom tries to lift you, but he's as weak as you. He leaves you on the ground, whispering, "Good luck, friend."

After just a few minutes, you hear harsh voices speaking Japanese above you. You open your eyes. A Japanese officer and guard look down at you and smile.

Too late, you realize your mistake. The officer nods to the guard. The guard removes his pistol from its holster and aims it at your head. He fires twice.

38

THE END
To follow another path, turn to page 11.
To read the conclusion, turn to page 101.

You decide to rest. You lie down in a clearing and quickly fall asleep.

A bright light wakes you. An Asian soldier stands over you, pointing his rifle at your head. He asks in English who you are. You give him your name and rank. He lowers his rifle.

"My name is Emilio," he says. "I am a Filipino fighter. I'll take you to our camp."

Other soldiers who fled the fort are at this jungle hideout. You decide to join the guerrillas and fight the Japanese.

Life as a guerrilla isn't easy. Danger and death are always near. But you have hope one day the war will end, and the Philippines will once again be free. And on that day you will return home.

THE END

To follow another path, turn to page 11.
To read the conclusion, turn to page 101.

Bernard Montgomery (forefront) became one of the most famous generals of World War II.

CHAPTER 3

SHOWDOWN IN THE DESERT

It is October 23, 1942. You are a British soldier in the 8th Army stationed in the Egyptian desert. Your commander is General Bernard Montgomery. You are stationed just outside the desert town of El Alamein, 60 miles west of the city of Alexandria. The Germans are dug in at El Alamein. The 8th Army's job is to drive them out.

The British have been fighting the Germans and their Italian allies in North Africa for two years now. German commander Field Marshal Erwin Rommel has again and again outsmarted previous British commanders. But Montgomery, or Monty as he is known to his troops, has a plan to beat him.

41

Turn the page.

Control of North Africa is important for both sides. If the Germans reach the Suez Canal in Egypt, they can control the flow of oil from the Middle East. The oil will fuel their tanks and other vehicles. Holding the Suez Canal will also give Germany control of North Africa and bring them closer to a final victory.

British Prime Minister Winston Churchill has been urging Monty for months to attack Rommel at El Alamein. But Monty won't be rushed. He spent all of September and most of October training new recruits. He has also trained you and other soldiers to defuse the thousands of land mines the Germans have scattered in the desert.

Monty also had his troops build dummy tanks, equipment, and soldiers in the south. He hopes these decoys will fool the Germans into thinking the attack will be there. But the real attack will be farther north.

Monty is ready for battle. The timing is good. Rommel is in Germany recovering from a stomach illness. The Germans won't have the "Desert Fox" to lead them.

The day of the attack is here. You know how to clear the mines. You also had some training in tank driving before you joined the infantry. But men to fight on the ground are needed too. How will you help?

• To work with the mine-clearing crew, turn to page 44.

• To drive a tank, turn to page 46.

• To march with the foot soldiers, turn to page 48.

Engineers had the grueling task of searching for mines hidden in the desert.

Your job is to go ahead of the tanks and clear a path for them into El Alamein. The minefields stretch 5 miles across and 40 miles long. There are at least 500,000 mines buried here. Rommel calls it the "Devil's Gardens."

There is no way your crews can defuse all these mines. Your goal is to clear a path 24 feet across, big enough for two tanks to pass.

Your partner, Jim, pulls out his mine detector. When the electric coils in the detector pass over a metal mine, it's supposed to sound a signal.

Jim looks up from his detector. "It's not working," he says. Neither is yours.

This isn't surprising. Many of the detectors aren't working properly. Some soldiers use their bayonets to look for mines. They poke the long knives that are attached to their rifles into the ground. But you're not sure you want to do that. If you stabbed a mine, it could explode.

"We can get new detectors when the supply truck comes by," you tell Jim.

"We can't wait," he replies. "The tanks are coming, and we've got to clear a path for them."

45

• To use your bayonet, turn to page 51.

• To wait for new detectors, turn to page 64.

You approach the tank you'll be driving. It is a Sherman tank, one of 300 newly arrived from the United States. It's the best tank in the world. Its long-barreled guns can outshoot every Axis tank except the German Panzer IVs. And Rommel only has about 30 of those.

Your tank joins a hundred others lining up on the desert road to El Alamein. The tanks move at a snail's pace, following the marked path of the minesweepers. This is going to be a long night.

The flow of tanks slows to nearly a standstill. It is one huge traffic jam. The tanks must stay behind the minesweepers, and that is causing the tie-up.

Suddenly you hear a buzzing noise over the roar of the tank.

"What's that noise?" you ask.

One of your crewmates pokes his head out of the tank.

"German planes are everywhere!" he shouts. "They're dropping bombs on the supply trucks."

Being stuck in this line makes your tank an easy target for the German artillery gunners. You don't have permission to leave the tank line. But if you stay where you are, you may be bombed at any moment.

47

• To cut out on your own, turn to page 52.

• To stay in line, turn to page 54.

You serve as a foot soldier. At 9:40 p.m. October 23, the order is given for the gunners to open fire on the German front. The sound of almost 900 artillery guns firing at once is deafening. Soon after the firing begins, Monty gives your unit the order to move forward.

You go before the tanks and most of the minesweepers. There is little danger of mines going off under your feet. It will take the weight of the tanks to set most of them off. That may be one reason why Monty has called this plan Operation Lightfoot.

You move forward through the smoke of battle. Within a few minutes, you're dodging bullets. You and your fellow soldiers drop to the sand. Up ahead you see the gunfire is coming from a foxhole. It is full of German soldiers.

You have two grenades in your pack. You could toss one of them at the foxhole. But the explosion may hurt Allied soldiers who are in the area. It might be better to get a little closer and fire on the foxhole with your rifle.

The smoke from the battle made it almost impossible for soldiers to see what was in front of them.

49

• To toss the grenade, turn to page 50.

• To get closer and shoot, turn to page 66.

You pull the pin and hurl the grenade at the foxhole. It explodes, and then the foxhole is silent.

Cautiously you move forward. Three soldiers lie dead in the foxhole. Several fellow infantrymen slap you on the back for a job well done. But you feel no satisfaction killing these men.

Then your radio crackles. "Retreat!" says a voice from headquarters. Operation Lightfoot has hit a snag. Soldiers around you start heading back to the start line. You feel numb about what you have just done. You need some time alone to think. But orders are orders.

50

- To head back with the others, turn to page 56.

- To hang back for a few moments, turn to page 67.

You decide not to waste time waiting for a new detector. You reach for your rifle and search for mines with your bayonet. You slice through the sand with the shiny blade. Jim does the same with his. Suddenly you strike something hard.

"I think I've found one," you say.

The two of you scrape away the sand. There is the mine. You begin to carefully remove the fuse. But the fuse is unfamiliar. You're not sure how best to remove it.

It might be better to leave the fuse as it is. But it could also be dangerous to move the mine with an intact fuse. Jim is just as unsure of what to do.

• To leave the fuse in the mine, turn to page 65.

• To try to defuse the mine, turn to page 69.

51

"Let's get out of here," you tell the other crew members.

"Right, mate," says Pete, the gunner. "We're just sitting ducks here."

You pull out of line and plow over the markers that show the safe road. You charge full speed ahead into the darkness.

You're almost to the front when suddenly you hit a mine. The tank is rocked by the explosion and stops dead in its tracks. Fire outside the tank quickly spreads inside. You throw open the hatch and leap out, your clothes aflame. You roll on the ground, putting out the fire.

You and your crewmates are all alive. But you've lost your tank. You're on foot in the midst of the battle.

52

Your first thought is to find another tank and hitch a ride. But your crewmate Steve doesn't agree.

"Better to hike it back to home base," Steve says. "We can get another tank there."

But you know it's unlikely you'll get another tank. Too many tanks have already been lost in this battle.

"There won't be room to ride in another tank," Steve reasons.

Your other crewmates side with Steve. But you still think getting on another tank might be safer than walking through a minefield.

53

• To try to hitch a ride, turn to page 55.
• To walk back to base, turn to page 68.

You take your chances and stay where you are in the unending line of tanks. You are lucky. The German artillery does not hit you or the other tanks in your caravan, although you have some close calls. Hours pass, and you make little progress. The cool desert night gives way to a blinding dawn.

Finally your radioman gets a signal. All tanks are recalled to base.

There were no roads to travel on in the desert. Tanks struggled over sand dunes and rocky plateaus.

54

Turn to page 56.

Hitching a ride on another tank is your best bet. At first you walk blindly in the desert darkness. Then the German bombs exploding overhead light the way to the tank caravan. Although they roll forward slowly, you're not sure they will see you. So you step dangerously close to the tanks' path. You pull off your shirt and wave it in the air to catch their attention.

But they don't see you in time. Before you can jump out of the way, you are hit by an oncoming tank. Unable to stop, the tank rolls over you, crushing every bone in your body. You are one of the first victims of the battle of El Alamein. And you're one of the few to be killed by your own side.

55

THE END

To follow another path, turn to page 11.
To read the conclusion, turn to page 101.

You arrive safely back at base camp. You return to the barracks for some sleep and wonder what the next day will bring.

It is the morning of October 26. You learn that German General Georg Stumme, who is commanding while Rommel is sick, is missing. Later you hear that his car was hit by British gunfire, and he suffered a fatal heart attack.

Rommel has been ordered back to the field from Germany to take command. Despite fighting hard, the Germans are in bad shape. They are low on fuel and supplies.

But Monty is taking no chances. In a few days he has come up with a new battle plan to drive the enemy out of El Alamein.

Monty reveals his new plan, called Operation Supercharge. Rommel is expecting you to attack again in the north. But Monty decides to surprise him with a major assault farther south. This time Monty will throw everything at the Germans at once—tanks, guns, and infantry.

You are eager to be a part of the action. Again, you have a choice. Both tank drivers and foot soldiers are needed.

Rommel (center) returned to El Alamein to find his troops losing the battle.

• To join the foot soldiers, turn to page 58.

• To command a tank, turn to page 61.

You have had enough of tanks. Your buddies in your infantry unit are glad to see you again. You begin the march into enemy territory. The minesweepers have done their work well, and you move quickly.

More than a week of bombing has left the Germans in bad shape. The farther you march, the more signs you see of defeat. Axis tanks and trucks litter the desert sands. There are bodies everywhere.

Suddenly, out of the smoke, you spy a group of four Germans on foot. They are carrying one of their wounded on a stretcher. It is your job to take them prisoner.

"Halt!" you cry out. But they only quicken their pace. "Halt or I'll shoot!" you cry again.

The retreating Germans are not stopping, despite your warning. You feel you have no choice but to fire. But can you do it?

59

• To shoot the Germans, turn to page 60.

• To hold your fire, turn to page 62.

You aim at the man in the rear of the group and shoot. He cries out and falls to his knees. The others put down the stretcher and open fire on you. You are hit twice in the leg and collapse to the ground. The Germans run away as your fellow soldiers surround you. Now you are the one who needs carrying.

By the time they get you back to the start line, you have lost a lot of blood. The British win the Battle of El Alamein, but you end up losing a leg.

60

THE END
To follow another path, turn to page 11.
To read the conclusion, turn to page 101.

You return to the tank division. Monty gives the order, and the tanks move forward. The Germans open fire. Many tanks around you burst into flames.

As the battle rages, a sandstorm hits. It offers protection from the enemy. The down side is that you can't see where you're going.

When the sandstorm finally dies down, you and your crew find yourselves in the open desert. You use maps and a compass to try to find the way back. Finally the gunner pokes his head out the hatch and yells, "Straight ahead! El Alamein!"

The town is in ruins. German forces have fled. You are disappointed to have missed the action but are grateful to be alive.

THE END
To follow another path, turn to page 11.
To read the conclusion, turn to page 101.

You can't bring yourself to fire. You watch the Germans disappear over the dunes. Perhaps they will be shot or captured by other British soldiers. But whatever happens, their blood won't be on your hands.

More tanks and trucks pass you on the road into El Alamein. Several of them stop and pick up you and your comrades. As you ride along, a jeep drives past at high speed. Sitting next to the driver is Monty. He is wearing a brightly colored scarf and waves at you and the others. There's a big grin on his face.

"Monty looks happy that we've won," says the driver of your truck.

"I bet Rommel isn't smiling right now," you say with a laugh.

In the days that follow, you realize how much this victory cost. Around 25,000 Germans and Italians have been killed or wounded. But at least 13,000 Allied troops were killed or wounded too.

You realize you're lucky to be alive. You hope your luck holds and the war ends soon.

British troops celebrated after winning the battle for North Africa.

THE END
To follow another path, turn to page 11.
To read the conclusion, turn to page 101.

You tell Jim you feel getting another detector is safer. He doesn't agree, but lets you have your way.

After a few minutes, the supply truck pulls up nearby. You begin to move toward it. "That's all right," says Jim. "I'll get it."

He heads toward the truck. BOOM! When the smoke clears, you see Jim lying on the ground, bathed in blood. He stepped on a small mine, the kind that can be tripped by a footstep.

Your friend is dead. It could have been you lying there. You will never forget this moment as long as you live.

64

THE END
To follow another path, turn to page 11.
To read the conclusion, turn to page 101.

You decide to leave the fuse alone. You don't want to accidently blow up the mine.

You carefully put the mine down on the ground. When the supply truck comes by, you can load it inside and have it brought back to base. There an expert can look at it.

As the supply truck comes rumbling toward you, a German shell whizzes down from the sky. It hits the mine, and the mine explodes. It kills you, Jim, and the driver of the truck. You never knew what hit you.

65

THE END
To follow another path, turn to page 11.
To read the conclusion, turn to page 101.

You crawl on your belly over the desert sand. A helmet peeks out of the foxhole. You stop and fire. The helmet disappears from sight. Did you hit the soldier under the helmet? You crawl closer to investigate. You feel a blazing pain as a bullet tears into your shoulder. You fire back. All is quiet in the foxhole.

You crawl closer and peer down into the foxhole. Below, a German soldier is lying still. Another is standing, clutching his side. You lock eyes, sharing a rare moment as two wounded soldiers, not as enemies. Soon British medics will bring help to both of you. For you and this German, the battle of El Alamein is over.

THE END
To follow another path, turn to page 11.
To read the conclusion, turn to page 101.

You don't want to be with the others, so you hang behind. You turn away from the soldiers you have killed, your mind filled with dark thoughts. Suddenly you feel a sharp pain in your side. You look down and see blood seeping from a wound. A soldier you thought you killed has just stabbed you with his bayonet. You turn your rifle on him and shoot. He slumps down, dead.

You are bleeding badly. You yell for help, but no one can hear you in the noise of battle. You suddenly feel very sleepy. In a few minutes, you fall into a sleep from which you will never wake.

67

THE END

To follow another path, turn to page 11.
To read the conclusion, turn to page 101.

It's a long and dangerous walk back to the base, but you make it safely before midnight. Lieutenant Jones, who sent you on this mission, is surprised to see you. You tell him what you did and what happened to your tank.

"Leaving the tank line was reckless and directly disobeying orders," he says. "You are a disgrace to your uniform."

Lieutenant Jones' words cut through you like a knife. You want to protest but can't find the words. You strike out with your fists instead. "Arrest that soldier!" cries the officer. You are hustled away and later court-martialed. You are sentenced to eight months in an Egyptian prison for striking an officer. The 8th Army goes on to win the battle of El Alamein, but you lose your freedom.

THE END
To follow another path, turn to page 11.
To read the conclusion, turn to page 101.

68

You can't leave the mine as it is. You have to defuse it.

Slowly you undo the fuse, bit by bit. Jim holds his breath as he watches you work. When the fuse is off and the mine is inactive, you both breathe a deep sigh of relief.

"That's another one down," Jim says.

You laugh at his remark. He grins back. This is just one mine out of hundreds that you and the other crews will disarm in the days to come. You are doing your part to clear a path for the tanks and foot soldiers to go forth into victory.

69

THE END

To follow another path, turn to page 11.
To read the conclusion, turn to page 101.

General Eisenhower (left) told soldiers, "Full victory—nothing else" before the June 6 invasion.

CHAPTER 4

INVASION AT NORMANDY

It is 4 a.m., June 6, 1944. You are on a ship in the English Channel between southern England and the northern coast of France. You are just one of about 130,000 soldiers waiting on the more than 5,000 ships.

You are part of the first wave of an Allied invasion to drive the Germans out of France. They have occupied France for four years.

Before you left England, American General Dwight Eisenhower addressed you and the other soldiers. "You are about to embark upon the Great Crusade," he said. Eisenhower is commander of the Allied forces in Europe and has been planning this invasion for months.

71

Turn the page.

The invasion was supposed to have taken place the day before. But bad weather caused a delay. Now as you look out at the choppy waters of the channel, you wonder how much the weather has improved.

Soon you and the other men move onto landing craft for the final leg of the trip. You will land on a beach in Normandy, France, code-named Omaha Beach. The boats are small. You feel the rolling waves much more than you did on the larger ship. Around you men are vomiting into little paper bags. You are feeling slightly sick yourself.

A strange silence falls over the boat as the shore comes into sight. You are about a quarter mile from land.

What awaits you on shore? Allied planes have been bombing the coast for weeks to drive the Germans back from the beaches. Maybe there will be no enemy waiting for you when you land. But that might be wishful thinking.

The shore looms closer. Men are getting nervous. Some are ready to jump into the water and wade to shore. Some of the men say if you wait until the beach to get off, you will be sitting ducks for German gunners on shore. Maybe they're right. You watch several soldiers leap into the water. Should you join them?

73

• To wait to get off, turn to page 74.

• To get off now, turn to page 76.

You'll stay on the landing craft until it gets closer to shore. You see many of the men who jumped off struggle in the deep water. You're glad you waited.

But as you get closer to the beach, you see German gunners firing. The coxswain in charge of the boat turns pale.

"You better get off now," he says to you and the other soldiers still on board.

"We can't," you reply. "We're still too far from shore. You need to get closer."

"I'm not going to risk my life," he says. "Get off. I'm turning this boat around."

The coxswain is endangering all your lives. But there's no time to argue with him.

You move to take control of the boat from the coxswain. He pushes you away. You come back at him and slug him in the stomach. He crumples to the deck. Six soldiers pin him down.

It's up to you now to bring the boat close enough to the beach so you and the other soldiers can get off. The only trouble is that you've never driven a boat before.

Tension was high for the troops on landing craft before the Normandy invasion.

Turn to page 80.

You put down your pack and rifle before entering the water. The deep water washes over your head.

Some of the men who got off can't swim. They splash helplessly in the water. One man seems to be drowning. You're a good swimmer and could possibly save him. But if you do, you will expose yourself to more German gunfire from shore.

- To swim to shore now, go to page 77.

- To help the drowning soldier, turn to page 78.

You decide not to help the drowning soldier. You feel bad about it, but you've got to think of your own safety. You swim toward shore with strong, swift strokes.

Suddenly water splashes wildly around you. The Germans are shooting at you from the beach!

If you dive underwater you'll be less of a target. But how long can you hold your breath? When you come up for air, you'll still be a target. Maybe it's better to keep your head above water so you can see what's coming.

77

• To keep your head above water, turn to page 83.

• To swim underwater, turn to page 84.

You swim to the drowning soldier. In his panic, he grabs you around the neck.

"Take it easy, or you'll drown us both!" you shout.

Your words calm him, and he loosens his grip. You wrap one arm around his shivering body and swim with your other arm. Slowly you move through the choppy waves.

The Germans on the beach have opened fire, but you manage to make it to land safely with your waterlogged friend. He has recovered and rushes up the sand behind you.

German soldiers are lined up along the plateau that looks over Omaha Beach. They fire machine guns, rifles, and bigger artillery at the soldiers below—at you. Everywhere you look there is confusion, smoke, and blood.

Soldiers who arrived ahead of you are struggling to get out of the line of fire. They are scrambling up the steep bluffs below the plateau. Then you notice a tank headed up the beach. Maybe you could run beside the tank for cover. But climbing to the plateau would get you off this dangerous beach.

79

• To climb to the plateau, turn to page 82.

• To hide by the tank, turn to page 85.

You gun the landing craft's engine. It leaps forward and speeds up the beach, coming to a sudden stop in the sand. You and the soldiers rush off, with the coxswain scrambling after you.

There are no other beached landing craft in the area. But there are plenty of other abandoned vehicles—tanks, transport ships, and supply units. But it's the bodies that make you stop. There are lots of soldiers, some dead, others wounded or dying, scattered along the beach. You are stunned, too dazed to move. Bullets zing all around you.

More than 34,000 U.S. troops landed on Omaha Beach on June 6, 1944.

Suddenly an officer runs up to you and the other men. You recognize him from the ship. He is Colonel George Taylor.

"Listen to me, men," he shouts above the noise of battle. "Two kinds of people are staying on the beach, the dead and those who are going to die. Now let's get the heck out of here!"

You get the message and follow Colonel Taylor up the beach to higher ground. You scramble up a steep bluff to the plateau above. You are lucky. There are no Germans there.

Some soldiers head in the direction of a nearby village. Others are going out into the countryside. Either way, you're likely to meet more Germans.

• To enter the French village, turn to page 93.

• To go into the countryside, turn to page 95.

81

You follow other soldiers up toward the plateau. The bluffs look difficult to climb, but you have no choice if you are going to get off the beach. In all the smoke and confusion, you get separated from the other soldiers as you climb.

Suddenly you hear low voices speaking in German. You have stumbled upon an enemy machine gun nest. They are picking off the Americans landing on the beach. You think you can skirt around them and continue up toward the plateau. But if you can take out the German nest, you could save many lives below.

• To continue to the plateau, turn to page 90.

• To attack the machine gun nest, turn to page 92.

You keep swimming with your head up. You're almost to shore when you feel a sharp pang in your shoulder. You've been hit. Another bullet strikes your leg. You struggle to keep your head above water, but the pain of your wounds is too much. As you watch the boats draw close to the beach, you sink to the bottom of the sea like a stone.

83

THE END

To follow another path, turn to page 11.
To read the conclusion, turn to page 101.

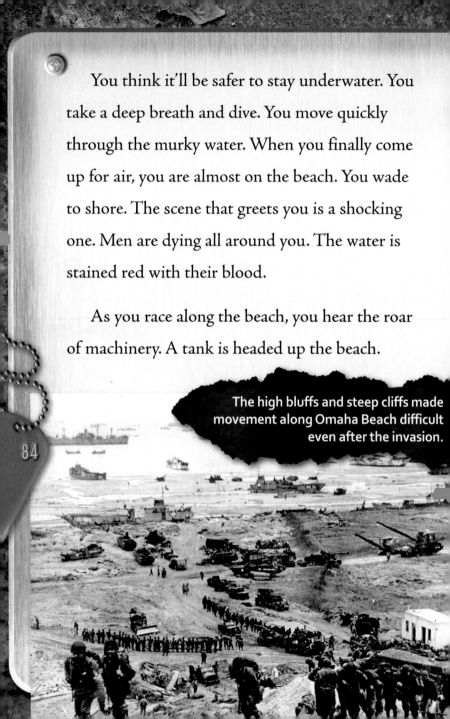

You think it'll be safer to stay underwater. You take a deep breath and dive. You move quickly through the murky water. When you finally come up for air, you are almost on the beach. You wade to shore. The scene that greets you is a shocking one. Men are dying all around you. The water is stained red with their blood.

As you race along the beach, you hear the roar of machinery. A tank is headed up the beach.

The high bluffs and steep cliffs made movement along Omaha Beach difficult even after the invasion.

You run alongside the tank, hoping it will offer some protection from the flying bullets.

The tank rolls up the beach. But suddenly the tread slips off, and the tank comes to a halt. The crew climbs out of the disabled tank. They head for the bluffs ahead and the plateau above them.

At either end of the beach are cliffs towering more than 100 feet. Some soldiers head for the cliffs, even though they appear far more difficult to climb than the bluffs. But German soldiers are firing from atop the bluffs. The cliffs, although a steeper climb, might not have Germans waiting to shoot you.

• To climb the cliffs, turn to page 86.

• To climb the bluffs, turn to page 88.

The cliffs are rocky, wet, and slippery. It's hard to get a grip as you climb. At times you feel yourself starting to slip, but you manage to hold on and keep going. A friend from your unit, Mike, is beside you. The two of you continue to slowly struggle up the cliff face.

Soldiers climbed the steep cliffs using only their hands or tiny rope ladders.

As you climb, Mike turns to you with a worried look on his sweaty face.

"I don't think I can make it," he gasps.

"We're almost there," you tell him. "You just have to hold on a little longer."

The top of the cliff is almost within reach when you hear Mike cry, "Help! I'm slipping!"

You turn to see his panic-filled face.

"Grab my hand," you tell him.

Mike puts out his hand. You lean down to grab it, but as you do, he falls. You watch in horror as he tumbles downward. Mike's final scream echoes in your ears—and it will for the rest of your life.

87

THE END

To follow another path, turn to page 11.
To read the conclusion, turn to page 101.

The path up the bluff is blocked with barbed wire and rocks that you and the other soldiers carefully walk around. You're worried the Germans have planted mines on the bluff, but you find none.

The top of the bluff is in sight. In a few moments you will be on the plateau. You pray that you will face no Germans there.

Your prayers go unanswered. A unit of German soldiers with rifles awaits you. They open fire. You leap into the air, and a bullet strikes your leg. Other men fall around you. Some of them are clearly dead. You are only wounded. But you lie still, hoping the Germans will take you for dead too.

They have no time to make sure you're dead. Their leader is barking orders. You open one eye and see them retreat from the advancing Allied forces. You continue to play dead until they are out of sight. Then you get up and look at the dead soldiers that surround you. You are bleeding and unable to walk. Soon the medics come and bandage your wound. You realize you're lucky to be alive.

89

THE END
To follow another path, turn to page 11.
To read the conclusion, turn to page 101.

You decide taking on the Germans alone is too risky. You quietly sneak around them, looking for a better place to continue climbing the bluff. But the bluffs are crawling with Germans. You can't find a clear path.

High cliffs tower over both ends of the beach. You head toward the cliffs. Some of the men from your unit are here, starting the dangerous upward climb on these 100-foot cliffs. Among them is your best friend, Ray.

"Be careful," Ray says when you arrive at the foot of the cliffs. "One misstep and you could fall and break your neck."

"Well, that's a better way to go than at the end of a German gun," you reply.

You both laugh, relieving the tension you feel. Then you begin to climb.

The top of the cliff is almost within reach when your hands begin to slip on the rocks. "Help!" you cry. Ray puts out his hand. Your hands are sweaty, but somehow you manage to hold onto your friend. Finally you get your grip on the rock again. You take a quick look down and breathe a sign of relief. The rocks below almost became your grave.

THE END

To follow another path, turn to page 11.
To read the conclusion, turn to page 101.

You reach into your pack and lift out one of four grenades you have been issued. In your nervousness, you drop the grenade. It starts to roll down the sandy slope. You run to retrieve it.

You pick up the grenade and pull the pin. But you wait a moment too long to hurl it at the Germans. It explodes in your hand.

The explosion blows away your hand and part of your arm. You lie bleeding on the ground. The Germans in the gun nest hear the explosion. They aim their machines guns at you and quickly put you out of your misery.

THE END
To follow another path, turn to page 11.
To read the conclusion, turn to page 101.

You join the other soldiers heading for the village. It is only a few miles away. When you reach it, the village is strangely quiet.

"The villagers must have fled when the Germans started bombing," says a soldier.

You walk down a street and see other American soldiers preparing to leave the village.

"We have orders to go to the town of St. Lo," one soldier tells you. "The Germans are holed up there. It should be some battle."

You're not ready to fight another battle. It'd be nice to stay here in the village for a while. But you may be needed to fight the Germans in St. Lo.

• To rest in the village, turn to page 94.

• To join the soldiers headed for St. Lo, turn to page 98.

93

You need a rest. You and some other soldiers find a deserted shop and fill up on fresh bread and cheese. Then you walk into a nearby field. The field is green, and the air you breathe is fresh and clean.

As you walk, you see an elderly Frenchman across the field waving wildly at you. You wave back. Now he is crying out to you in English. "Watch out!" he cries. "Mines!"

You stop in your tracks, but not soon enough. The field is loaded with small German mines that are easily triggered by a man's weight. You step on one and it explodes, killing you instantly.

THE END

To follow another path, turn to page 11.
To read the conclusion, turn to page 101.

You head out for the countryside. A few miles down the road, you come to a stone farmhouse. A woman rushes out the door.

"American?" she says in a French accent.

"*Oui*," you say. It is one of the few French words you know.

She hugs you and speaks rapidly in French. Her name is Emilie. She takes you inside and introduces you to her husband, Henri.

As Emilie prepares you a meal, there is a knock at the door. A harsh voice says something in German.

The couple motions for you to hide in their bedroom. But your first instinct is to run out the back door.

• To hide in the house, turn to page 96.

• To escape out the back, turn to page 99.

You follow Henri into the bedroom. He pulls clothes from a dresser. You change and shove your uniform into a drawer. Just then the door opens, and a German officer enters. He asks you something in French. You say nothing and pretend to be putting clothes away.

Emilie comes to your rescue. She points to her ear as she jabbers in French. She is telling the officer that you are deaf.

The German stares at you for a long time. Then he seems to accept her story and leaves. You breathe a sigh of relief.

As soon as the officer and his men have left, Emilie gives you some food wrapped in a cloth. Then the couple sends you on your way. You will never forget their kindness.

The Germans are in full retreat from Normandy now. You link up with your unit and continue to advance south. On August 25, 1944, you enter the French capital of Paris. The Germans have fled.

The people of Paris celebrate your arrival. There is music and dancing in the streets. It seems a lifetime ago since you landed on Omaha Beach. The invasion that so many soldiers gave their lives for has succeeded. The Germans have lost nearly all the territory they held for four years. It can't be long before the war is over.

97

THE END

To follow another path, turn to page 11.
To read the conclusion, turn to page 101.

You join the soldiers marching to St. Lo to fight the Germans. It is a long trip. St. Lo is not far, but the Germans are everywhere. They fight your advance through the countryside. You spend weeks in a soggy field, waiting for more Allied troops to join you. On July 11 you close in on St. Lo, and the battle begins.

The fighting is fierce, but the town falls to the Allies in about a week. The Germans retreat. Much of St. Lo has been reduced to rubble, but victory is yours.

You are transferred to the 4th Division, which is marching farther northeast toward the capital city of Paris. You arrive there in about six weeks. The Germans have fled. Paris is free. The end of the war is near, and you can't wait to go home.

98

THE END
To follow another path, turn to page 11.
To read the conclusion, turn to page 101.

You are afraid of being caught in the house. You rush out the back door. Angry voices call to you in German. You run faster. You hear shots and feel a stab of pain in your side. You stumble and fall.

In moments, two German soldiers with rifles are standing over you. They are quickly joined by their officer. He barks a command and the two soldiers lift you to your feet. Other soldiers return to the farmhouse. You hear shots and cries. Emilie and Henri have paid for their kindness with their lives.

The Germans will be moving out to keep ahead of the invading Americans. And you will go with them as a prisoner of war.

THE END

To follow another path, turn to page 11.
To read the conclusion, turn to page 101.

Infantrymen used tanks for cover as they marched into towns.

CHAPTER 5

THE WAR ENDS AT LAST

World War II lasted more than six years. Eventually the Allies pushed the Axis powers out of the countries they had invaded. The infantrymen who battled on the ground were a main reason the Allies won the war.

The infantry made great sacrifices, fighting and dying in one major battle after another. Infantrymen were killed and wounded. Others were captured and held as prisoners of war. Still others went missing in action. Of the U.S. Army casualties in the war, about 80 percent were suffered by the infantry. The 3rd Infantry Division alone reported nearly 26,000 casualties.

101

Infantrymen were sent into battle again and again during the war. The average foot soldier faced 45 days of combat, but some units and divisions were under fire for longer. The 32nd Infantry Division, which served in the Pacific, was in combat for 654 days. In combat or out of it, infantrymen were away from their homes and loved ones for a long time.

For many, gunfire wasn't the only threat to their health. Many infantrymen fought in extreme conditions—the hot, burning sands of North Africa or the steamy, humid jungles of the Pacific islands. Others suffered frigid cold in parts of Europe.

The infantry's sacrifices helped the Allies to victory over the Axis powers. The British Army's powerful assault of foot soldiers and tanks on El Alamein, Egypt, drove the Germans out of Egypt. That battle effectively ended the Germans' hopes of conquering North Africa.

American and Filipino soldiers weren't able to stop the Japanese from taking the Philippines. But they showed great courage on the Bataan Death March and in the terrible Japanese prison camps. News of cruelties committed in these places made the Allies more determined than ever to defeat the Axis powers.

The massive invasion of Normandy on D-Day soon drove the Germans out of France. This victory paved the way to the end of the war.

The infantry's strength and courage were demonstrated in hundreds of other battles throughout the war. British infantry landed in Sicily off the coast of Italy in July 1943 and took the entire island in just 39 days. During this time Mussolini fell from power, and the Italians surrendered to the Allies.

Allied infantry faced stiff resistance in the Battle of the Bulge. In the Ardennes Forest of Belgium and France, the Germans made a last stand in December 1944. The Allies were driven back by 38 German divisions, until British armored units broke through the enemy lines from the south. By January 1945 the U.S. infantry had recovered every bit of land lost to the Germans.

U.S. infantrymen looked for any hidden
enemies in Waldenburg, Germany,
near the end of the war.

The infantry's efforts freed millions of people
worldwide. It took years for war-torn nations to
recover. But without the infantry and its sacrifices,
that recovery might never have happened. Men on
foot, armed with only a few weapons and brave
hearts, won the war and changed the world.

TIMELINE

1922—Benito Mussolini becomes prime minister of Italy.

1933—Adolf Hitler comes to power in Germany.

May 1939—Hitler and Mussolini sign the "Pact of Steel," a pact for world domination.

September 1, 1939—Germany invades Poland. Two days later Great Britain and France declare war on Germany, setting off World War II.

June 22, 1940—France falls to Germany, following several other Western European nations.

December 7, 1941—The Japanese launch a sneak attack on the U.S. naval base at Pearl Harbor, Hawaii.

December 8, 1941—The United States declares war on Japan.

February 22, 1942—U.S. General Douglas MacArthur withdraws from the Philippines.

April 1942—Thousands of American and Filipino soldiers surrender to the Japanese on the Bataan Peninsula.

May 1942—The Battle of Corregidor ends in a Japanese victory; about 650 American prisoners of war die on the Bataan Death March.

October 23, 1942—The battle of El Alamein begins, pitting the British against the Germans in the Egyptian desert.

November 1, 1942—General Bernard Montgomery launches the final phase of the battle, Operation Supercharge; within days the Germans under Field Marshal Erwin Rommel are in retreat.

June 6, 1944—The Allies launch a massive invasion of the Normandy coast of German-occupied France.

August 25, 1944—The Allies free Paris.

December 1944–January 1945—Germany makes a last stand in Belgium at the Battle of the Bulge.

April 30, 1945—Hitler commits suicide in his bunker in Berlin, Germany; Germany surrenders a week later.

August 6–9, 1945—American planes drop atomic bombs on the Japanese cities of Hiroshima and Nagasaki.

September 2, 1945—Japan officially surrenders, bringing World War II to an end.

OTHER PATHS TO EXPLORE

In this book you've seen how the events experienced by World War II infantrymen look different from three points of view.

Perspectives on history are as varied as the people who lived it. You can explore other paths on your own to learn more about what happened. Seeing history from many points of view is an important part of understanding it.

Here are some ideas for other World War II points of view to explore:

+ Filipinos fought side by side with Americans in the Philippines. But unlike their allies, they were fighting for their homeland. How was their war experience different?

+ During the war German leader Adolf Hitler had millions of European Jews killed. What was the war like for these people?

+ American women were not allowed to be soldiers in World War II. But many of them served their country in other ways, both at home and abroad. What was their war experience like?

READ MORE

Rose, Simon. *The Split History of World War II: A Perspectives Flip Book*. North Mankato, Minn.: Compass Point Books, 2013.

Samuels, Charlie. *Timeline of World War II: Europe and North Africa*. New York: Gareth Stevens Pub., 2012.

Stein, R. Conrad. *World War II*. New York: Children's Press, 2012.

INTERNET SITES

Use FactHound to find Internet sites related to this book. All of the sites on FactHound have been researched by our staff..

Here's all you do:

Visit *www.facthound.com*

Type in this code: 9781429699648

GLOSSARY

artillery (ar-TIL-uh-ree)—large guns, such as cannons or missile launchers, that require several soldiers to load, aim, and fire

barracks (BEAR-uhks)—housing for soldiers

bluff (BLUFF)—a tall, steep bank or cliff

casualty (KAZH-oo-uhl-tee)—someone who is injured, captured, killed, or missing in an accident, a disaster, or a war

court-martial (KORT-MAR-shuhl)—a trial for members of the military accused of breaking rules or committing a crime

coxswain (KOK-swayn)—a sailor who usually steers a boat and is in charge of the boat's crew

evacuate (i-VA-kyuh-wayt)—to leave a dangerous place and go somewhere safer

guerrilla (guh-RIL-ah)—a member of a small group of fighters or soldiers

malaria (muh-LAIR-ee-ah)—a disease that causes fever and chills; it is spread by the bite of mosquitoes that carry the disease

plateau (pla-TOH)—an area of high, flat land

BIBLIOGRAPHY

Ambrose, Stephen E. *D-Day June 6, 1944: The Climactic Battle of World War II.* New York: Simon & Schuster, 1994.

Baldwin, Hanson W. "The Fall of Corregidor." *American Heritage,* August 1966, 16-23, 84-90.

Cawthon, Charles R. "July 1944, St. Lo." *American Heritage,* June 1974, 4-11, 82-88.

Collier, Richard. *The War in the Desert. World War II.* Alexandria, Va.: Time-Life Books, 1977.

Hastings, Max. *Victory in Europe: D-Day to V-E Day.* Boston: Little, Brown, 1985.

Lewis, Jon E., ed. *The Permanent Book of the 20th Century: Eye-Witness Accounts of the Moments that Shaped Our Century.* New York: Carroll & Graf, Pub., 1994.

McCormick, Ken, and Hamilton Darby Perry, eds. *Images of War: The Artist's Vision of World War II.* New York: Orion Books, 1990.

Sulzberger, C.L. *The American Heritage Picture History of World War II.* New York: American Heritage Pub. Co., 1966.

INDEX

Allies, 7, 11, 31, 37, 49, 71, 73, 101, 103, 107

Axis powers, 7, 11, 101, 103

Bataan Death March, 17, 18–19, 20, 21, 22–23, 24, 26–27, 28, 32, 37, 38, 103, 106

battles in Europe, 11, 104
  Battle of the Bulge, 104, 107
  Normandy invasion (D-Day), 70–92, 97, 103, 107
  St. Lo, 93, 98

battles in North Africa, 11
  El Alamein, 41–69, 103, 107

battles in the Pacific Ocean, 11, 102
  Bataan peninsula, 12, 13, 14, 31, 106
  Corregidor island, 16, 36, 106

casualties, 63, 80, 97, 101

causes of World War II, 7–8

Churchill, Winston, 42

Eisenhower, Dwight, 70, 71

Filipino guerrillas, 31, 39

Hitler, Adolf, 8, 9, 10, 106, 107

MacArthur, Douglas, 13, 31, 106

minefields, 42, 43, 44–45, 48, 51, 52, 53, 58, 64, 65, 69, 94

Montgomery, Bernard, 40, 41, 42, 56–57, 61, 62, 107

Mussolini, Benito, 8, 9, 104, 106

Omaha Beach, 72, 97
  bluffs on, 79, 81, 82, 84, 85, 88, 90
  cliffs on, 84, 85, 86–87, 90–91
  plateaus on, 79, 81, 82

Operation Lightfoot, 48, 50

Operation Supercharge, 57, 107

Pearl Harbor, 10, 106

prison camps, 17, 20, 21, 27, 28, 29, 32, 103

prisoners of war, 17, 21, 26, 29, 32–33, 37, 99, 101, 106

Rommel, Erwin, 41, 42, 43, 56, 57, 62, 107

tanks, 43, 46–47, 52–53, 54–55, 57, 58, 61, 68, 79, 84–85

Taylor, George, 81

Wainwright, Jonathan, 14, 15, 16

4-13